TYPE *IN* PLACE

A Thumbnail Approach to Creative Type Placement

BY

RICHARD EMERY

ROCKPORT PUBLISHERS • ROCKPORT MASSACHUSETTS
Distributed by North Light Books • Cincinnati, Ohio

First published in the United States of America by:
Rockport Publishers, Inc.
P.O. Box 396
Five Smith Street
Rockport, Massachusetts 01966
Telephone: (508) 546-9590
Fax: (508) 546-7141
Telex: 5106019284 ROCKORT PUB

Distributed to the book trade and art trade in the U.S. by:
North Light, an imprint of
F&W Publications
1507 Dana Avenue
Cincinnati, Ohio 45207
Telephone: (513) 531-2222

First Canadian edition 1992, published by
Rockport Publishers, Inc. for
Firefly Books Ltd.
250 Sparks Avenue
Willowdale, Ontario M2H 2S4
Telephone: (416) 499-8412
Fax: (416) 499-8313

First Taiwan edition 1992, published by
Rockport Publishers, Inc. for
Long Sea International Book Co., Ltd.
No. 29, Lane 3, Linyi Street
Taipei, Taiwan R.O.C.
Telephone: (02) 394-6497-8
Fax: 886-2-3968502

First Korean edition 1992, published by
Rockport Publishers, Inc. for
Chunghan Bookstore
#107 Subway Shopping Center
Kangnom Express Bus Terminal
Banpo-dong, Secho-gu
Seoul 137 040 Korea
Telephone: (02) 533-6790, 535-1709
Fax: (02) 535-5470

ISBN 0-935603-87-5
Printed in Hong Kong

ACKNOWLEDGEMENTS

This project came to full reality through the efforts
of many people, but I must begin by acknowledging
Don Traynor for planting the first seed.
This was the spur that set
things in motion.

Thanks to Stan Patey for his support and
encouragement, and special thanks to
Ken Pfeifer for his contribution of time and
creative thinking.

Finally I am grateful and honored for the
thoughtful introduction by Primo Angeli who took
time from his busy schedule to comment
on type placement and the
purpose of this book.

STAFF & CONTRIBUTORS

EDITOR/DESIGNER..........Richard Emery
ART ASSISTANT..........Karen Shea

Cover Photo: David Benoit

Contents

Introduction

Type arrangement may be the most important graphic element in design. The reason for this is simple: Typography carries many messages. But there is more to the subject than this. Type can work with graphic imagery to become a visual message that in turn carries a verbal message. Executed correctly, typography can be well-integrated into an overall design and appropriately consumed by the reader as a complete functional aesthetic entity. Or, it could look like an imposition, an afterthought with unrelated incongruous features, an interference to language.

Type placement is more than typography or type design. Type design is a more detail-oriented subject that does not effect a design as globally as does type placement. Type placement deals less with the actual typeface and more with the configuration of type. Good arrangement of type depends on the relative sizes of type and how blocks of text fit together in relation to the rest of a design. Therefore, type placement is design with the shapes formed by type. The terms "type placement" and "type arrangement" may be used interchangeably for our purposes.

Type placement concerns the use of space around the typography to elicit different moods and effects.

What might appear to the untrained eye as unused space surrounding the typography may in fact be a style that releases the message from the constriction of "busyness" and makes it more accessible to the reader and the content easier to consider. "White Space," as this is often called, creates a comfort for the eye that makes the reader more responsive to reading the message.

Taking this style 180 degrees, it can be considered that a rectangle full of typography and graphics gives the impression of abundance and plenty, and awards the reader the sense that somewhere amid all the "busyness" there has to be something of value. This is also a perfectly legitimate and proven approach.

All this discussion is attempting to convey is that type placement is an activity of mood setting and message enhancement. This gives a certain power to the designer that should not be overlooked. The best piece of graphic art can have its effect negated by poorly considered type placement. Conversely, through the power of placement, the combination of graphics and type can express the perfect visual message and achieve the results desired when the project was first introduced.

Thus certain configurations of type can evoke certain aesthetic feelings. A short line length of tall type can work quite well for an attention-getter or for a quick identification. In the same way, a longer line length of smaller type can look more elegant and subtle. For this example, only one may suit the design. Depending on the particular piece, both or neither may work.

Designers make use of type placement in a problem-solving stage of design. Of course, every designer approaches a job a little differently, and each may approach each job a little differently, but there always comes a time when the problem of type arrangement must be considered. Designers need freedom and flexibility in making these decisions. Examples of other successful arrangements are a great help, and this book is an accessible addition to such a repertoire.

Richard Emery's TYPE IN PLACE is a book by which designers may start from scratch, without starting from the point of imitation. The acetates, used in conjunction with the book, are a natural way to creatively approach type arrangement because they work with you in thumbnail. By using these materials, you have the tools to solve type arrangements as an alternative to imitation.

Primo Angeli is the Principal of Primo Angeli Inc., a San Francisco-based marketing design firm.

How to Use this Book

The intent of this book is to provide the graphic designer with a quick and easy tool for visualizing in thumbnail the many combinations and possibilities of type placement. We present here a variety of sizes and shapes to facilitate image selection. First we have selected five common area shapes (6x9 vertical; 7x10 vertical; 7x4 3/4, half-page horizontal; 2 3/8 x 10, 1/3 page vertical; 8 1/2 x 11 vertical). Within these size formats we offer three choices on the amount of design area covered by the photography, art or color (full coverage; 1/2 area covered; 1/4 area covered). These combinations offer the designer a chance to experiment with combinations of overprint, white reverse, and combinations of type within and without the art area. The book is divided into three general categories: color photography, black and white photography and areas of solid color. The color areas are each labeled for the exact combination of process-color screens used.

Attached to the back inside cover is a pocket that contains acetates with opaque type forms. These acetates show various sizes and shapes of headline and body (text) type and can be combined to simulate numerous combinations of sizes in both black and white. Thus by placing these opaque type forms over the design areas provided, the designer can easily visualize in thumb-nail any idea under consideration.

In the pocket there are eleven acetates. They are labeled to correspond to the five area shapes. By placing these acetates over the art that most resembles the design being considered, the designer can explore all the many possibilities available until an approximation results. Thus the designer can immediately translate what was visualized in thumbnail to what is intended at full size. Example: if a white headline and an area of black body type are being considered, the designer selects the acetate of white headlines and the acetate of black body type and experiments with all the different possibilities on each sheet.

DIAM IT AMET, IPSCING ABORE ONUMY SED

This is a block of copy to show how to place type. When you use all of the many varieties of size suggestions you will then be able to design and place copy to best utilize the design that you have in mind. Remenber that the type presented here is only for placement and does not mean to show type style. Placement has a very important role to play in the process of graphic design. The use of type placement can give mood and attitude an to any graphic area and deliver the desired results. When you use type to present a specific mood you must recognize that there are many aspects to be considered. One of them is the concept of defining who will be the consumer of this product or promotion. When this has been decided you can determine if you want to use type placement in a way that shows a style consistent with the market that you have determined. This is often misunderstood by a

This is a block of copy to show how to place type. When you use all of the many varieties of size suggestions you will then be able to design and place copy to best utilize the design that you have in mind. Remenber that the type presented here is only for placement and does not mean to show type style. Placement has a very important role to play in the process of graphic design. The use of type placement can give mood and attitude an to any graphic area and deliver the desired results. When you use type to present a specific mood you must recognize that there are many aspects to be considered. One of them is the concept of defining who will be the consumer of this product or promotion. When this has been decided you can determine if you want to use type placement in a way that shows a style consistent with the market that you have determined. This is often misunderstood by a the designer. Sometimes crowded and busy placements can give an

Gadipscing

Clropsmoy onp bsgno tufa

attitude of great quantity and ample and supply, whereas a clean and open placement can give an attitude of elegance and refinement. There are many gradations of attitude between these two extremes and the designer must decide which is the most appropriate for the project being considered. It is also true that sometimes the opposite placement can have the effect of underscoring the mood by implication. This is somewhat of a touchy position to task a the designer must take on the responsibility of the decision of this implication. Another way that type place-

the designer. Sometimes crowded and busy placements can give an attitude of great quantity and ample and supply, whereas a clean and open placement can give an attitude of elegance and refinement. There are many gradations of attitude between these two extremes

Manp of hes lubbl on plem!

Fupz
LOREM IPSUM DOLOR

This is a block of copy to show how to place type. When you use all of the many varieties of size suggestions you will then be able to design and place copy to best utilize the design that you have in mind. Remenber that the type presented here is only for placement and does not mean to show type style. Placement has a very important role to play in the process of graphic design. The use of type placement can give mood and attitude an to any graphic area and deliver the desired results. When you use type to present a specific mood you must recognize that there are many aspects to be considered. One of them is the concept of defining who will be the consumer of this product or promotion. When

GREAT

PLACEMENTS

Type placement is a varied and flexible process. In fact, that is exactly what this book is all about. When the designer begins to relate typography with photography and/or art there can be an overwhelming sense of the possibilities. Yet the designer is restricted only by the limits of the imagination.

In the following pages we have collected an assortment of excellent examples of type usage, especially in the way that type is placed within the rectangle. We have examined many wonderful presentations and because of the restrictions of space cannot include them all. But we present to you the following as prime examples of how

type can be creatively placed within a rectangle, especially a rectangle that is also occupied by other elements such as art or photography. The opportunity to see beautiful and successful displays of type placement is both an educational and an inspirational experience.

GREAT PLACEMENTS is an important way to access this design tool. It affords an opportunity for the designer to begin the creative process through observation even before actual placement begins. We know you will be inspired, and we hope you will find many opportunities to use this process for your own creative needs.

We accept full responsibility for the way these people look.

Design Firm: Mullen
Client: Puma
Art Director: John Doyle
Photographer: John Huet

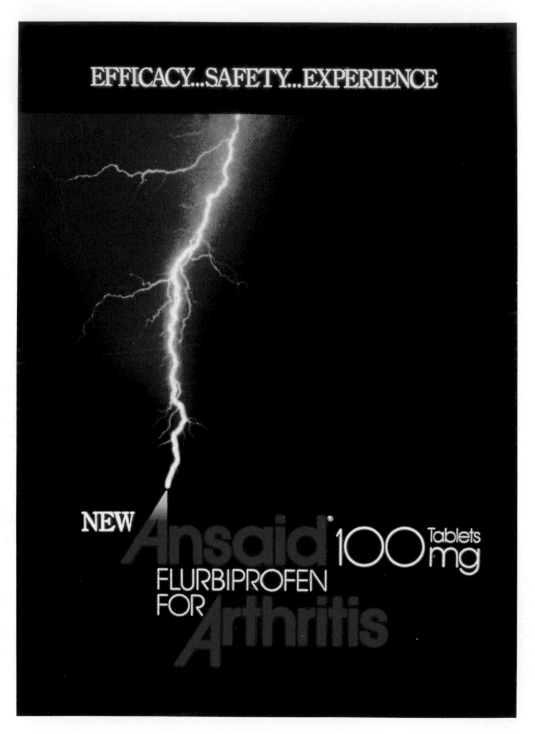

Design Firm: Kallir, Philips, Ross, Inc.
Product: Ansaid
Client: The Upjohn Company
Art Director: Gerald Philips
Photographer: Stock

Design Firm: Mullen
Client: McCormack & Dodge
Art Director: Brian Fandetti
Photographer: Al Fisher

Design Firm: Cosmopulos, Crowley, & Daly, Inc.
Product: Salvation Army
Client: Salvation Army
Art Director: Starvos Cosmopulos/Bruce Hurwit
Photographer: George Petrakes

Design Firm: Tyler Smith Design
Product: Mens Clothing
Client: Southwick
Art Director: Tyler Smith
Photographer: Myron

Design Firm: Kallir, Philips, Ross, Inc.
Product: Innovar
Client: McNeil
Art Director: Martin Minch
Photographer: Bernard Lawrence

Design Firm: Mullen
Client: Puma
Art Director: John Doyle
Photographer: Myron

Just because the game is old, doesn't mean there aren't new ways to play it.

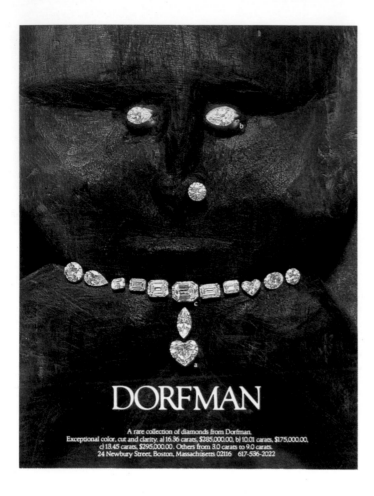

Design Firm: Cosmopulos, Crowley, & Daly, Inc.
Product: Diamonds
Client: Dorfman Jewlers
Art Director: Starvos Cosmopulos/Richard Kerstein
Photographer: Onofiro Paccione

Design Firm: Hill, Holliday Advertising
Product: The Boston Globe
Client: The Boston Globe
Art Director: Jamie Mambro, Richard Foster
Photographer: Mike Ryan

Design Firm: Kallir, Philips, Ross, Inc.
Product: Tylenol
Client: McNeil
Art Director: Bruce Tredwell

L O U I S

Design Firm: Tyler Smith Design
Product: Mens Retail Store
Client: Louis, Boston.
Art Director: Tyler Smith
Photographer: Myron

S P R I N G

S U M M E R

1 9 8 7

Design Firm: Mullen
Client: World Society for the Protection
of Animals
Art Director: John Doyle
Photographer: Clint Clemens

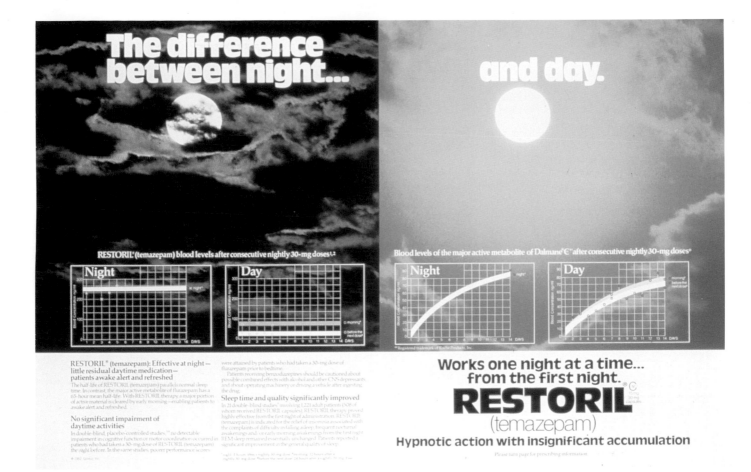

Design Firm: Kallir, Philips, Ross, Inc.
Product: Restoril
Client: Sandoz
Art Director: Jay Cohen
Photographer: Stock

Design Firm: Kallir, Philips, Ross, Inc.
Product: PAC
Client: Pharmaceutical Advertising Council
Art Director: John Geryak
Photographer: Stock

From thousands of seeds: a single flower

The prescription drugs dispensed in this pharmacy were developed by research-intensive pharmaceutical companies at a substantial investment in time and money. Thousands of compounds must be prepared and tested, over a period of more than 10 years, at an average cost exceeding $200 million, for any one medication made available for your doctor's prescription.

That's why prescription drugs are not cheap. But, by shortening the duration of illness, avoiding or reducing hospital costs, permitting a quicker return to productive work, and enhancing the quality of our lives, they are the most cost-effective part of all health expenditures.

PAC The Pharmaceutical Advertising Council, Inc.

Design Firm: Mullen
Client: Hit or Miss
Art Director: Margaret McGovern
Photographer: John Huet

Design Firm: Hill, Holliday Advertising
Product: Killington Ski Resort
Client: Killington, Vermont
Art Director: Jamie Mambro
Photographer: Hans Neleman

Design Firm: Tyler Smith Design
Product: Mens Retail Store
Client: Louis, Boston.
Art Director: Tyler Smith
Photographer: Stock

Design Firm: Cosmopulos, Crowley, & Daly, Inc.
Product: Fans
Client: Duracraft
Art Director: Starvos Cosmopulos, Richard Kerstein
Photographer: Gary Arruda

Design Firm: Richard Emery Design, Inc.
Product: Book Cover
Client: Little, Brown and Co.
Art Director: Richard Emery
Photographer: Emory Kristof

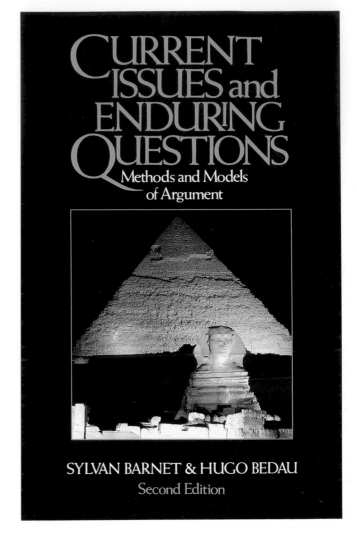

Design Firm: Mullen
Client: USTrust
Art Director: John Doyle
Photographer: Myron

Design Firm: Carson Design
Product: Book Cover
Client: Bedford Books *of* St. Martin's Press
Art Director: Sally Carson
Photographer: Bruce T. Martin

Design Firm: Kallir, Philips, Ross, Inc.
Product: Cleocin T Lotion
Client: The Upjohn Company
Art Director: Jim Walsh
Photographer: Claude Mougin

Traveling the world for the finest raw materials. Searching for the ultimate quality of cashmere in Chinese Mongolia. Fabrics and clothing of unparalleled softness and luxury . . . this is the Zegna dedication to quality.

I am Ermenegildo Zegna.

Ermenegildo Zegna Corporation, 9 W 57th St., New York, NY 10019 (212) 751-3468

Design Firm: Tyler Smith Design
Product: Mens' Clothing
Client: Ermenegildo Zegna
Art Director: Tyler Smith
Photographer: Myron

Design Firm: Mullen
Client: Puma
Art Director: John Doyle
Photographer: Myron

Design Firm: Hill, Holliday Advertising
Product: A. T. Cross Signature Line Pens
Client: A. T. Cross
Art Director: Nancy Wovers
Photographer: Hans Neleman

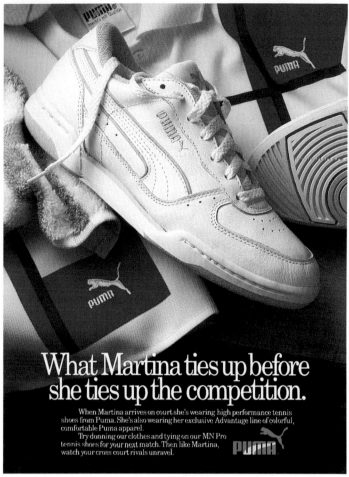

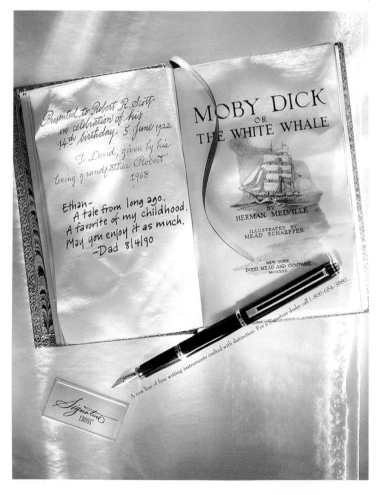

Design Firm: Hill, Holliday Advertising
Product: The Infiniti G20, M30, Q45
Client: Infiniti Division of
Nissan Motor Corp., USA
Art Director: Vic Cevoli
Photographer: Clint Clemens

Design Firm: Mullen
Client: Manchester League of Women Voters
Art Director: Margaret McGovern
Photographer: Stock photograph

Leaves and grass left out for the trash pickup go to a public incinerator, adding to the pollution index as well as your tax bill. Simple backyard composting can solve both problems. Find out more May 5 at Earth Care Fair, the Memorial School, 8:30 AM to 12:30 PM. Sponsored by the Manchester League of Women Voters and the Solid Waste Committee.

EARTH CARE FAIR, MAY 5. GARDENING. COMPOSTING. RECYCLING.

FALL 1991

JOSEPH
ABBOUD

Design Firm: Tyler Smith Design
Product: Apparel
Client: Joseph Abboud
Art Director: Tyler Smith
Photographer: Fabrizio Ferri

NOW AVAILABLE, THE COLORS OF YOUR MIND.

Imagine.

Suddenly before you is a color you had dreamed of, but never knew existed.

Not a halfhearted hybrid, but a living, vibrant color.

Imagine, furthermore, gazing at a profusion of newly discovered, totally fresh reds, blues, browns and yellows. In all, 700 of the purest, most brilliant colors ever seen outside of your own head.

These are the colors of Toyo Ink, part of a total color system so remarkable, over 90% of its available colors can be created from just 14 base inks, including the four process colors.

Every day, more printers discover it.

Every day, more art directors and designers insist on it.

They've learned what the Japanese have known for so long: What good is putting ink to paper if the color you see is not the color you first saw in your mind?

PIGMENTS OF THE IMAGINATION.

CCS·TOYO

Design Firm: Tyler Smith Design
Product: Printing Ink
Client: Toyo Ink
Art Director: Tyler Smith
Photographer: Clint Clemens

PIGMENTS OF THE IMAGINATION.

One shade of blue means sadness.

Another is coolness.

Another vastness.

Another emptiness.

How you see color in your mind is how Toyo Ink has been reproducing color since 1907.

Toyo's international success is not due entirely to its quality of color.

Nor is it a matter of Toyo's outstanding selection of colors, over 700 to date.

It is not even because Toyo ink prints so beautifully and easily on virtually any type of press.

It is the intelligence of the Toyo Ink System. Over 90% of the available colors can be created from just 14 base inks, including the 4 process colors.

All over the world, people insist on Toyo Ink and accept no substitutes.

After all, what good is putting ink to paper if the color you see is not the color you first saw in your mind?

CCS·TOYO

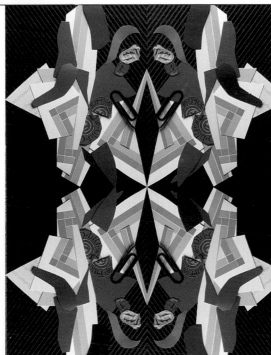

Design Firm: Tyler Smith Design
Product: Printing Ink
Client: Toyo Ink
Art Director: Tyler Smith
Photographer: Myron

Design Firm: Hill, Holliday Advertising
Product: Grand Hyatt Wailea Resort & Spa
Client: Hyatt Hotels Corporation
Art Director: Dick Pantano, Vic Cevoli
Photographer: Clint Clemens

Design Firm: Mullen
Client: Puma
Art Director: John Doyle
Photographer: John Huet

Design Firm: Mullen
Client: American Heart Association
Art Director: Amy Watt
Photographer: John Holt

Design Firm: Donovan and Green
Product: Book Jacket
Client: Rockport Publishers, Inc., Allworth Press
Art Director: Julie Riefler
Photographer: Ron Watts

Design Firm: PPI Marketing Group
Product: Commercial Space
Client: Boston Design Center
Art Director: Stephen Bridges
Photographer: Steve Rosenthal

Design Firm: PPI Marketing Group
Product: Software
Client: Micro Business Software, Inc.
Art Director: Stephen Bridges
Photographer: Bill Smith Studio, Inc.

Design Firm: Mullen
Client: Apollo
Art Director: John Doyle

Design Firm: Weymouth Design
Product: Coated Paper, Computer & Office
Supplies, Photofinishing Services
Client: Nashua Corporation
Photographer: Michael Weymouth

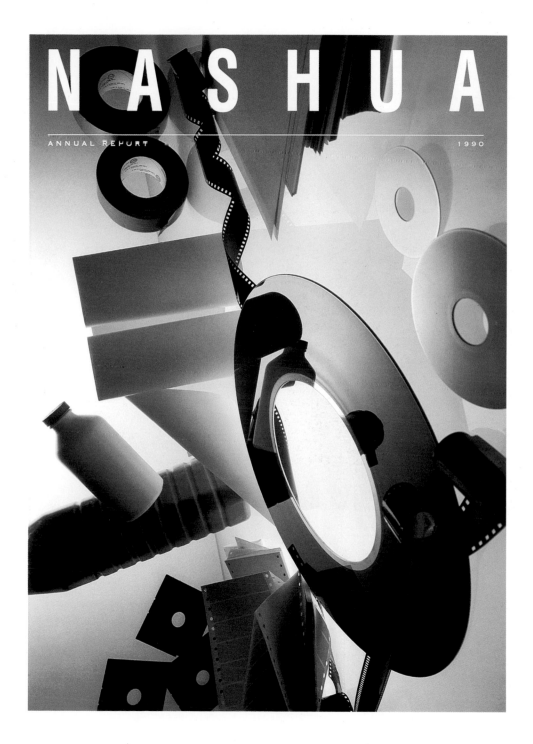

Proof that a four-session terminal is more productive than a two-session terminal.

Introducing the IDEA 177. A System 3X or AS/400 terminal that can actually double your productivity by making it possible for users to perform up to four tasks at once.

For example, a warehouse supervisor receives an order. With the IDEA 177's two host-addressable printer sessions and two simultaneous display sessions, he or she can check inventory, verify a customer's credit status, scan the product's serial number with a bar code reader and print shipping documentation all at the same time.

On the other hand, an insurance agent might concurrently enter a claim, check on prior claims, ascertain a customer's payment history, then print a letter to the local agent.

The possibilities are limitless. And so are the ways in which you can configure the IDEA 177. It features full 5219 emulation, and its two printer ports let you connect to virtually any PC printer.

You can use the serial port to take in data from magnetic stripe or bar code readers, and simultaneously print through the parallel port. The IDEA 177 even presents information in 80 or 132 columns, on your choice of color screens.

The IDEA 177. It's one terminal that can really nourish your appetite for greater productivity.

IDEA
The intelligence to do things better.

IDEA Courier   IDEAssociates   IDEA Servcom

Design Firm: Mullen
Client: IDEAssociates
Art Director: Margaret McGovern
Photographer: John Holt

Design Firm: Weymouth Design
Product: Microcomputer Products
Client: MicroAmerica Inc.
Art Director: Michael Weymouth
Photographer: Michael Weymouth

Design Firm: Mullen
Client: Pizzeria Uno
Art Director: Amy Watt
Photographer: David Bradshaw

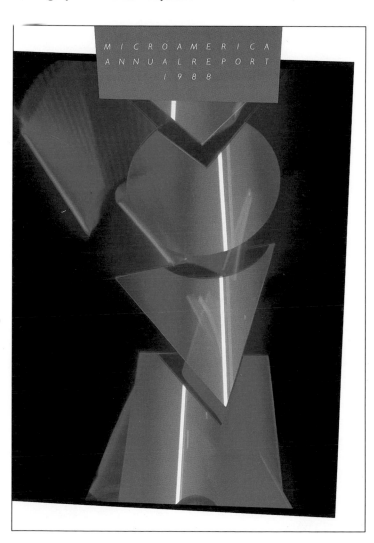

Design Firm: Kallir, Philips, Ross, Inc.
Product: Nursoy
Client: Wyeth
Art Director: John Geryak
Photographer: Nancy Brown

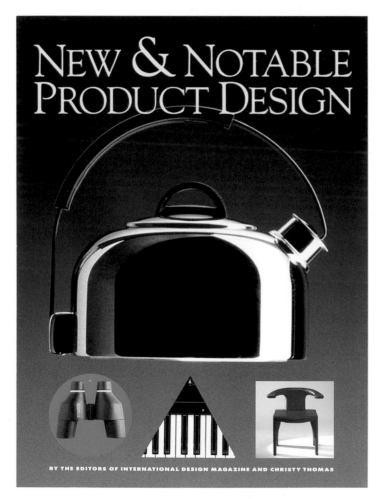

Design Firm: Rockport Publishers, Inc.
Product: Book Jacket
Client: Rockport Publishers, Inc.
Art Director: Stephen Bridges

Strong hints of masculine shaping dominate trenches both long and short, cropped blousons, swing coats, anoraks, duffles, wrap jackets, bathroom coats, and motocross biker shapes. Shaped from fit to flare, lengths vary from above the knee to longer lines. Fabric considerations draw selections of chenille "blanket" fabrics, clear plastic, slickers, vinyls, laces, leathers, ginghams, poplins, linens, mesh, flight silks, and appearances of embroidered fabrics. Coloration ranges from brights, pastels and black-and-whites to prints of fancies, iridescence, and metallics. Excitement is created with details of zippers, hardware trims, lace-ups, military pockets, jewel necklines, hoods, visors, and collar treatments.

Outerwear

Design Firm: Bridges Design
Product: Fashion Magazine
Client: Rockport Publishers, Inc.
Art Director: Stephen Bridges
Photographer: Roberto Rabanne

Design Firm: Mullen
Client: United Cerebral Palsy Assoc. of
Greater Boston
Art Director: Brian Fandetti
Photographer: George Petrakes

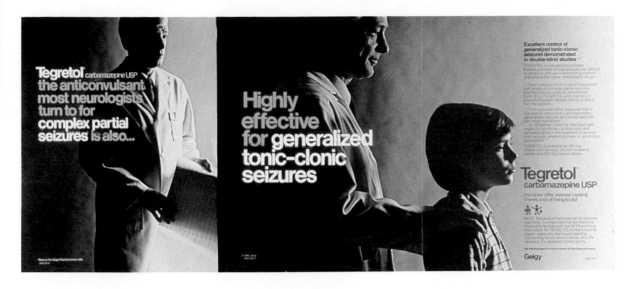

Design Firm: Kallir, Philips, Ross, Inc.
Product: Tegretol
Client: CIBA-Geigy
Art Director: Al Zalon
Photographer: Bernard Lawrence

Design Firm: Bridges Design
Product: Magazine Cover
Client: Rockport Publishers, Inc.
Art Director: Stephen Bridges
Photographer: Roberto Rabanne

Drexel Burnham Lambert

The investment banking and securities business is one of perpetual change. Making the right moves when everything is in constant motion requires the right instincts...instincts that many young people don't know they have until they put them to work. What we offer at Drexel Burnham Lambert is a tremendously diverse environment in which young people can sharpen these instincts and in the process begin a productive business career.

Design Firm: Weymouth Design, Inc.
Product: Investment
Client: Drexel Burnham Lambert
Art Director: Michael Weymouth
Photographer: John Goodman

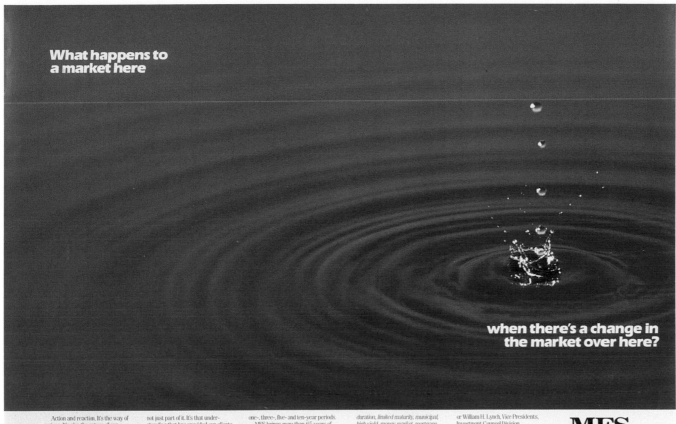

Design Firm: Cosmopulos, Crowley, & Daly, Inc.
Product: Money Markets
Client: Mass Financial Services
Art Director: Starvos Cosmopulos/Richard Kerstein
Photographer: Ed Braverman

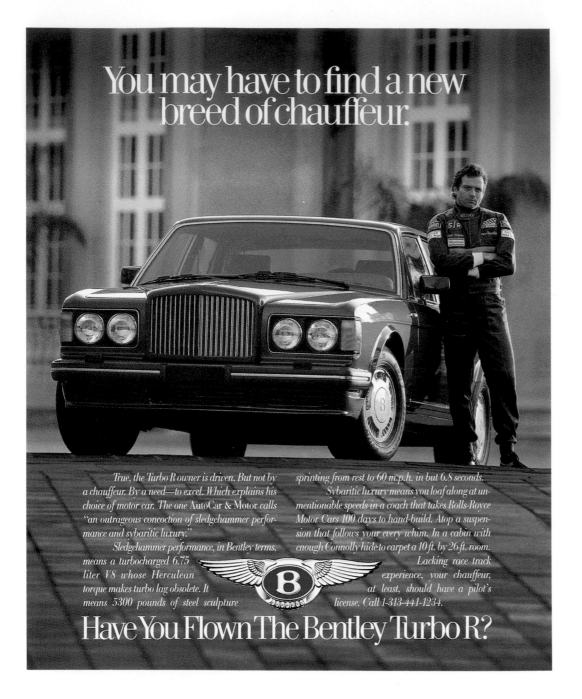

You may have to find a new breed of chauffeur.

True, the Turbo R owner is driven. But not by a chauffeur. By a need—to excel. Which explains his choice of motor car. The one AutoCar & Motor calls "an outrageous concoction of sledgehammer performance and sybaritic luxury."

Sledgehammer performance, in Bentley terms, means a turbocharged 6.75 liter V8 whose Herculean torque makes turbo lag obsolete. It means 5300 pounds of steel sculpture sprinting from rest to 60 m.p.h. in but 6.8 seconds.

Sybaritic luxury means you loaf along at unmentionable speeds in a coach that takes Rolls-Royce Motor Cars 100 days to hand-build. Atop a suspension that follows your every whim. In a cabin with enough Connolly hide to carpet a 10 ft. by 26 ft. room.

Lacking race track experience, your chauffeur, at least, should have a pilot's license. Call 1-313-441-1234.

Have You Flown The Bentley Turbo R?

Design Firm: Mullen
Product: Bentley
Client: Rolls-Royce Motor Cars, Inc.
Art Director: Brian Fandetti
Photographer: Clint Clemens

RUBBER CONSISTS OF LONG, RANDOMLY COILED CHAIN-LIKE MOLECULES WHICH PRODUCE ITS ELASTICITY. WHEN CARBON BLACK IS DISPERSED THROUGHOUT RUBBER, MICROSCOPIC AGGREGATES SUCH AS THOSE SIMULATED HERE INTERACT WITH THE RUBBER MOLECULE. THE OBSERVABLE EFFECT IS THAT THE RUBBER BECOMES STRONGER, OR HAS INCREASED "MODULUS". CARBON BLACK INCREASES THE USEFUL LIFE OF RUBBER ARTICLES BY PROVIDING INCREASED TENSILE STRENGTH, HARDNESS AND TEAR RESISTANCE. CARBON BLACK ALSO REDUCES THE TENDENCY OF RUBBER TO SWELL WHEN EXPOSED TO OILS AND GREASES AND FACILITATES EXTRUSION OF RAW RUBBER COMPOUNDS. A TIRE PRODUCED WITHOUT A REINFORCING AGENT WOULD LAST LESS THAN 1,000 MILES.

Design Firm: Weymouth Design
Product: Specialty Chemicals and Materials, Energy
Client: Cabot Corporation
Art Director: Michael Weymouth
Photographer: Larry Long

Design Firm: Cosmopulos, Crowley, & Daly, Inc.
Product: Shoes
Client: Maine Woods
Art Director: Starvos Cosmopulos/Bruce Hurwit
Photographer: George Petrakes

Design Firm: Kallir, Philips, Ross, Inc.
Product: Haldol
Client: McNeil
Art Director: Martin Minch

Design Firm: Kallir, Philips, Ross, Inc.
Product: Cleocin Phosphate
Client: The Upjohn Company
Art Director: Gerald Philips
Photographer: Sheldon Secunda

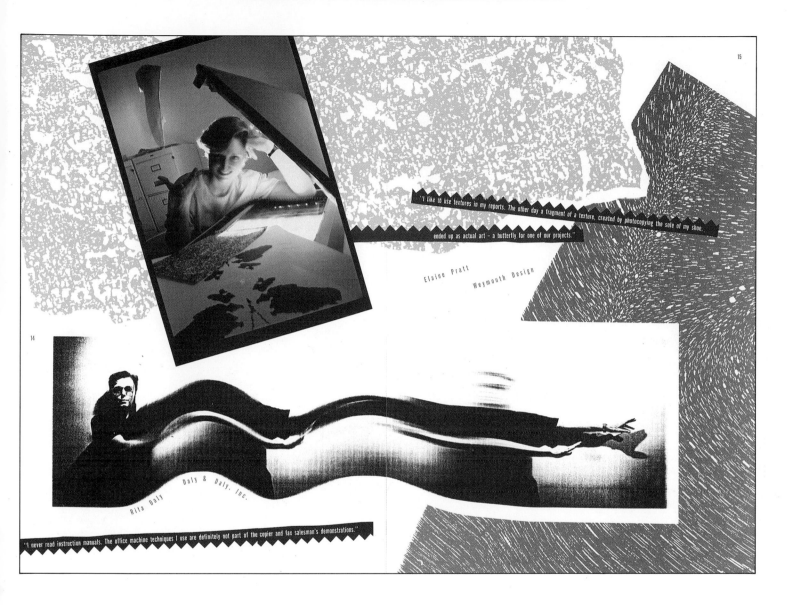

"I like to use textures in my reports. The other day a fragment of a texture, created by photocopying the sole of my shoe, ended up as actual art – a butterfly for one of our projects."

Elaine Pratt   Weymouth Design

Rita Daly   Daly & Daly, Inc.

"I never read instruction manuals. The office machine techniques I use are definitely not part of the copier and fax salesman's demonstrations."

Design Firm: Weymouth Design
Product: Paper
Client: Monadnock Paper Mills, Inc.
Art Director: Michael Weymouth
Photographer: George Simian

Design Firm: Bridges Design
Product: Fashion Magazine
Client: Rockport Publishers, Inc.
Art Director: Stephen Bridges
Photographer: Roberto Rabanne

Design Firm: Cosmopulos, Crowley, & Daly, Inc.
Product: New England Journal of Medicine
Client: New England Journal of Medicine
Art Director: Starvos Cosmopulos/Richard Kerstein
Photographer: Jim Conanty

SELECTOR

Now it is your turn. The following pages open up for you the world of type placement. These pages will not make design decisions for you, but they will present you with a field within which you may discover the appropriate size and placement for any idea you may have. Look for a picture or color that approximates what you have in mind. Choose the acetates that apply to your selection and begin the easy access to type placement. Once you have comfortably settled into this process we know that you will be using it freely and often.

This book is not intended to show type design in terms of the various type faces and fonts available. Instead we have selected a single popular face, helvetica, and displayed it for you in various sizes and shapes. We leave up to you the actual decisions on the specific type styles that will be appropriate for your idea.

So welcome to the TYPE IN PLACE design book.

The following 42 pages show full coverage color photography with opportunities for both black overprinted and white reverse type. Photographs on these two pages by **SuperStock,** *11 West 19th St., New York, NY 10011, 212-633-0300*

6x9 vertical

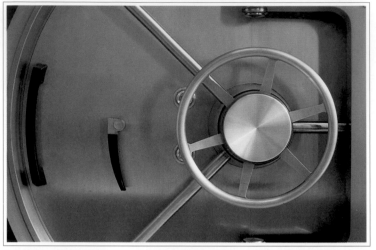

7x4 3/4, 1/2 pg. horizontal

7x10 vertical

2 3/8x10, 1/3 pg. vertical

8 1/2x11 vertical

6x9 vertical

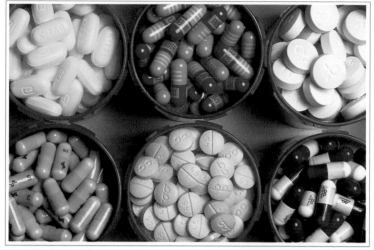

7x4 3/4, 1/2 pg. horizontal

7x10 vertical

2 3/8x10, 1/3 pg. vertical

8 1/2x11 vertical

Photographs on these two pages by **Rob Huntley,**
*Chromographics, Inc., 9 May St., Beverly, MA 01915,
508-927-7451*

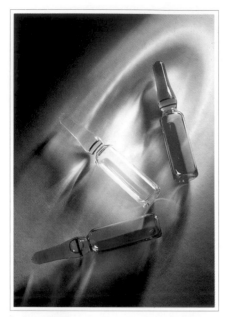

6x9 vertical

7x4 3/4, 1/2 pg. horizontal

7x10 vertical

2 3/8x10, 1/3 pg. vertical

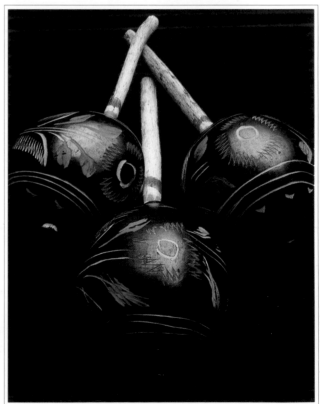

8 1/2x11 vertical

6x9 vertical

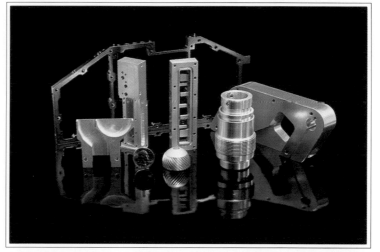

7x4 3/4, 1/2 pg. horizontal

7x10 vertical

2 3/8x10, 1/3 pg. vertical

8 1/2x11 vertical

Photographs on these two pages by **White/Packert Photography,** *107 South St., Boston, MA 02111, 617-423-0577*

6x9 vertical

7x4 3/4, 1/2 pg. horizontal

7x10 vertical

2 3/8x10, 1/3 pg. vertical

8 1/2x11 vertical

6x9 vertical

7x4 3/4, 1/2 pg. horizontal

7x10 vertical

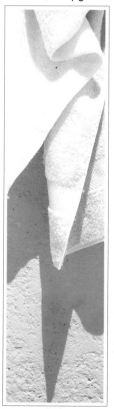

2 3/8x10, 1/3 pg. vertical

8 1/2x11 vertical

Photos on these two pages by **Eric Roth Photography,** *337 Summer St., Boston, MA 02210, 617-338-5358 Janet K. Henderson, Manager.*

6x9 vertical

7x4 3/4, 1/2 pg. horizontal

7x10 vertical

2 3/8x10, 1/3 pg. vertical

8 1/2x11 vertical

6x9 vertical

7x4 3/4, 1/2 pg. horizontal

7x10 vertical

2 3/8x10, 1/3 pg. vertical

8 1/2x11 vertical

Photographs on these two pages by **Terence O'Toole,**
Panorama Productions, 118 Social Hall Avenue,
Salt Lake City, UT 84111, 801-364-7482

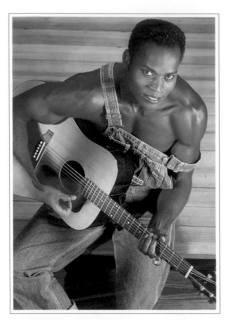

6x9 vertical

7x4 3/4, 1/2 pg. horizontal

7x10 vertical

2 3/8x10, 1/3 pg. vertical

8 1/2x11 vertical

6x9 vertical

7x4 3/4, 1/2 pg. horizontal

7x10 vertical

2 3/8x10, 1/3 pg. vertical

8 1/2x11 vertical

Photos on these two pages by **Paul Avis,** *300 Bedford St., Manchester, NH 03101, 603-627-2659 Represented by Jane Sutton*

7x4 3/4, 1/2 pg. horizontal

6x9 vertical

7x10 vertical

2 3/8x10, 1/3 pg. vertical

8 1/2x11 vertical

6x9 vertical

7x4 3/4, 1/2 pg. horizontal

7x10 vertical

2 3/8x10, 1/3 pg. vertical

8 1/2x11 vertical

*Photographs on these two pages by **Benoit Photography**,
31 Blackburn Center, Gloucester, MA 01930, 508-281-3079*

6x9 vertical

7x4 3/4, 1/2 pg. horizontal

7x10 vertical

2 3/8x10, 1/3 pg. vertical

8 1/2x11 vertical

7x4 3/4, 1/2 pg. horizontal

6x9 vertical

7x10 vertical

2 3/8x10, 1/3 pg. vertical

8 1/2x11 vertical

Photographs on these two pages by **Sandro Miller***, New View Studios, 5275 Michigan Ave., Rosemont, IL 60018, 708-671-0300*
Represented by Elizabeth Miller

6x9 vertical

7x4 3/4, 1/2 pg. horizontal

7x10 vertical

2 3/8x10, 1/3 pg. vertical

8 1/2x11 vertical

6x9 vertical

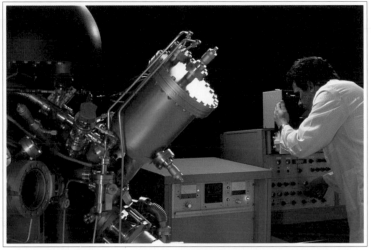

7x4 3/4, 1/2 pg. horizontal

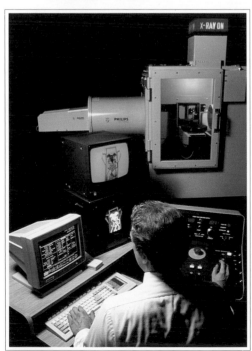

7x10 vertical

2 3/8x10, 1/3 pg. vertical

8 1/2x11 vertical

Photographs on these two pages by **Scott Payne,** *New View Studios, 5275 Michigan Ave., Rosemont, IL 60018, 708-671-0300*
Represented by Elizabeth Miller

6x9 vertical

7x4 3/4, 1/2 pg. horizontal

7x10 vertical

2 3/8x10, 1/3 pg. vertical

8 1/2x11 vertical

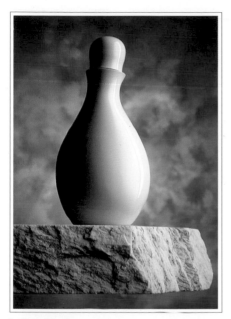

6x9 vertical

7x4 3/4, 1/2 pg. horizontal

7x10 vertical

2 3/8x10, 1/3 pg. vertical

8 1/2x11 vertical

Photographs on these two pages by **Rod Cook,**
New York, NY, 212-995-0100
Represented by Terry Dagrosa, 212-254-4254

6x9 vertical

7x4 3/4, 1/2 pg. horizontal

7x10 vertical

2 3/8x10, 1/3 pg. vertical

8 1/2x11 vertical

6x9 vertical

7x4 3/4, 1/2 pg. horizontal

7x10 vertical

2 3/8x10, 1/3 pg. vertical

8 1/2x11 vertical

Photographs on these two pages by **Rob Van Petten,** *109 Broad St., Boston, MA 02110, 617-426-8641*

7x4 3/4, 1/2 pg. horizontal

6x9 vertical

7x10 vertical

2 3/8x10, 1/3 pg. vertical

8 1/2x11 vertical

6x9 vertical

7x4 3/4, 1/2 pg. horizontal

7x10 vertical

2 3/8x10, 1/3 pg. vertical

8 1/2x11 vertical

Photographs on these two pages by **Dennis Gray** *, 8705 W. Washington Blvd., Culver City, CA 90232, 213-559-1711*

6x9 vertical

7x4 3/4, 1/2 pg. horizontal

7x10 vertical

2 3/8x10, 1/3 pg. vertical

8 1/2x11 vertical

6x9 vertical

7x4 3/4, 1/2 pg. horizontal

7x10 vertical

2 3/8x10, 1/3 pg. vertical

8 1/2x11 vertical

Photographs on these two pages by **Ken Sabatini,** *1112 Beachwood Dr., Los Angeles, CA 90038, 213-462-7744*

7x4 3/4, 1/2 pg. horizontal

6x9 vertical

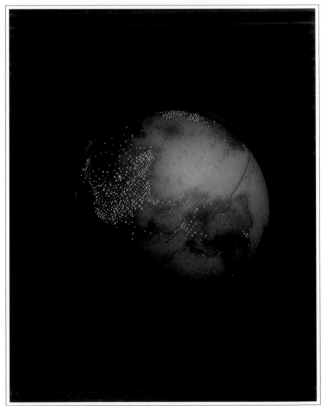

7x10 vertical

2 3/8x10, 1/3 pg. vertical

8 1/2x11 vertical

6x9 vertical

7x4 3/4, 1/2 pg. horizontal

7x10 vertical

2 3/8x10, 1/3 pg. vertical

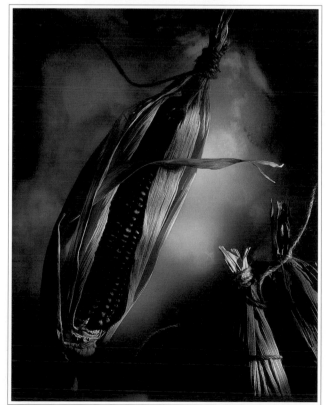

8 1/2x11 vertical

Photographs on these two pages by **SuperStock,** *11 West 19th St., New York, NY 10011, 212-633-0300*

6x9 vertical

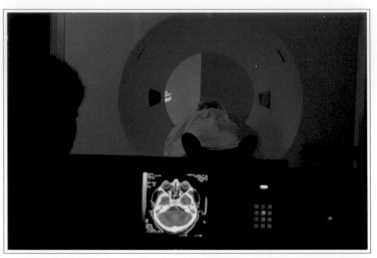

7x4 3/4, 1/2 pg. horizontal

7x10 vertical

2 3/8x10, 1/3 pg. vertical

8 1/2x11 vertical

6x9 vertical

7x4 3/4, 1/2 pg. horizontal

7x10 vertical

2 3/8x10, 1/3 pg. vertical

8 1/2x11 vertical

Photographs on these two pages by **Lorraine Parow,**
Toronto, CANADA, 416-461-3847

6x9 vertical

7x4 3/4, 1/2 pg. horizontal

7x10 vertical

2 3/8x10, 1/3 pg. vertical

8 1/2x11 vertical

6x9 vertical

7x4 3/4, 1/2 pg. horizontal

7x10 vertical

2 3/8x10, 1/3 pg. vertical

8 1/2x11 vertical

Photographs on these two pages by **Wayne Calabrese,** *CR2 Studios Inc., 36 St. Paul St., 601/The Cox Building, Rochester, NY 14604, 716-232-5140*

6x9 vertical

7x4 3/4, 1/2 pg. horizontal

7x10 vertical

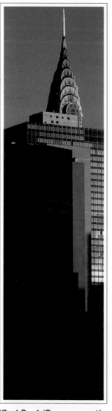

2 3/8x10, 1/3 pg. vertical

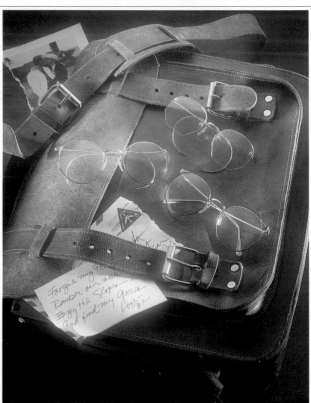

8 1/2x11 vertical

6x9 vertical

7x4 3/4, 1/2 pg. horizontal

7x10 vertical

2 3/8x10, 1/3 pg. vertical

8 1/2x11 vertical

Photographs on these two pages by **Clint Clemens.**
Represented by A Corporation for Art and Commerce,
212-206-0737, FAX 212-463-7267

6x9 vertical

7x4 3/4, 1/2 pg. horizontal

7x10 vertical

2 3/8x10, 1/3 pg. vertical

8 1/2x11 vertical

6x9 vertical

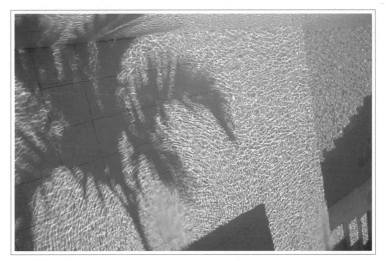

7x4 3/4, 1/2 pg. horizontal

7x10 vertical

2 3/8x10, 1/3 pg. vertical

8 1/2x11 vertical

Photographs on these two pages by **Susie Cushner Photography,** 354 Congress Street, Boston MA 02210
617-542-4070
Represented by Marilyn Cadenbach Associates
617-484-7437

6x9 vertical

7x4 3/4, 1/2 pg. horizontal

7x10 vertical

2 3/8x10, 1/3 pg. vertical

8 1/2x11 vertical

6x9 vertical

7x4 3/4, 1/2 pg. horizontal

7x10 vertical

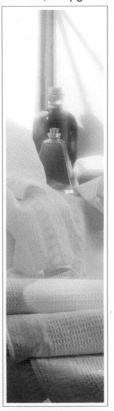

2 3/8x10, 1/3 pg. vertical

8 1/2x11 vertical

Photographs on these two pages by **John Huet Photography,** *27 Drydock Avenue, Boston, MA 02210*
617-439-9393
Represented by Marilyn Cadenbach Associates
617-484-7437

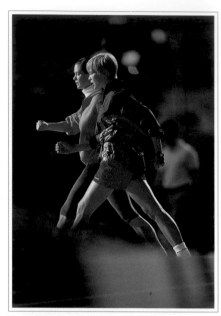

7x4 3/4, 1/2 pg. horizontal

6x9 vertical

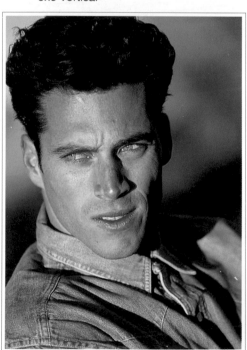

7x10 vertical

2 3/8x10, 1/3 pg. vertical

8 1/2x11 vertical

6x9 vertical

7x4 3/4, 1/2 pg. horizontal

7x10 vertical

2 3/8x10, 1/3 pg. vertical

8 1/2x11 vertical

Photographs on these two pages by **Geoffrey Stein Studio, Inc.,** *348 Newbury Street, Boston, MA 02115 617-536-8227*

7x4 3/4, 1/2 pg. horizontal

6x9 vertical

7x10 vertical

2 3/8x10, 1/3 pg. vertical

8 1/2x11 vertical

6x9 vertical

7x4 3/4, 1/2 pg. horizontal

7x10 vertical

2 3/8x10, 1/3 pg. vertical

8 1/2x11 vertical

Photos on these two pages by **SuperStock,**
11 West 19th St., N.Y., N.Y. 10011, 212-633-0300

6x9 vertical

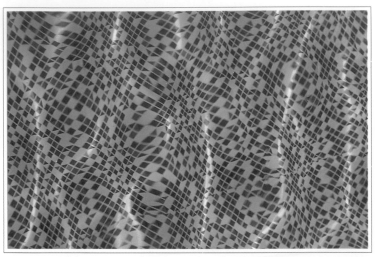

7x4 3/4, 1/2 pg. horizontal

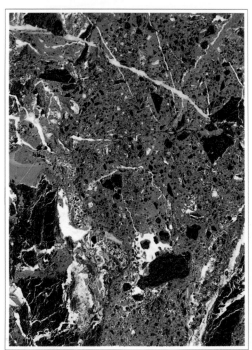

7x10 vertical

2 3/8x10, 1/3 pg. vertical

8 1/2x11 vertical

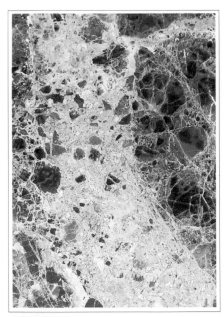

6x9 vertical

7x4 3/4, 1/2 pg. horizontal

7x10 vertical

2 3/8x10, 1/3 pg. vertical

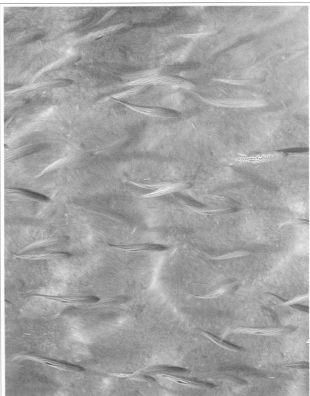

8 1/2x11 vertical

The following 6 pages show full coverage illustrations with opportunities for both black overprinted and white reverse type. Illustrations on this page are by **Gaylord Welker,** *30 Summit Rd., Sparta, NJ 07871, 201-729-5134*

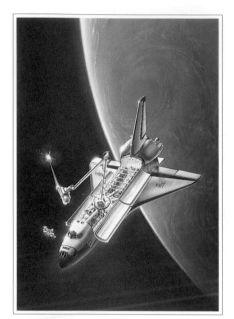

6x9 vertical

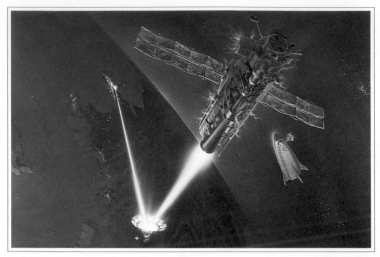

7x4 3/4, 1/2 pg. horizontal

7x10 vertical

2 3/8x10, 1/3 pg. vertical

8 1/2x11 vertical

Illustrations on this page by **Kirk Moldoff,**
Represented by Joanne Palulian, 18 McKinley St.,
Rowayton, CT 06853, 203-866-3734

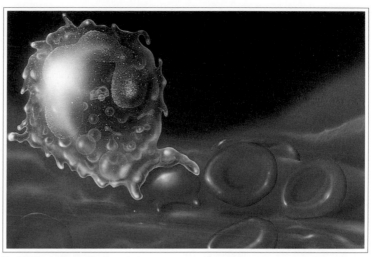

7x4 3/4, 1/2 pg. horizontal

6x9 vertical

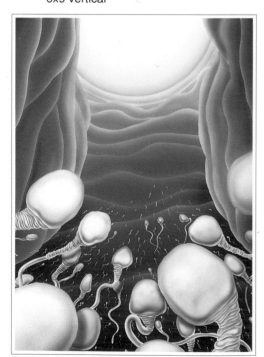

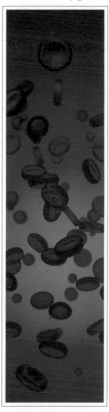

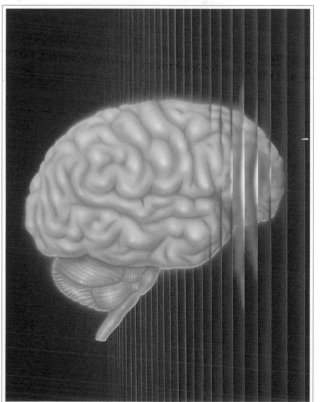

7x10 vertical

2 3/8x10, 1/3 pg. vertical

8 1/2x11 vertical

Illustrations on this page by **Dick Palulian,**
Represented by Joanne Palulian, 18 McKinley St.,
Rowayton, CT 06853, 203-866-3734

6x9 vertical

7x4 3/4, 1/2 pg. horizontal

7x10 vertical

2 3/8x10, 1/3 pg. vertical

8 1/2x11 vertical

Illustrations on this page by **Bob Conge,** *28 Harper St., Rochester, NY 14607, 716-473-0291*

6x9 vertical

7x4 3/4, 1/2 pg. horizontal

7x10 vertical

2 3/8x10, 1/3 pg. vertical

8 1/2x11 vertical

Illustrations on this page by **Gary Ruddell,** *875 Las Ovejas,*
San Rafael, CA 94903, 415-479-1010

6x9 vertical

7x4 3/4, 1/2 pg. horizontal

7x10 vertical

2 3/8x10, 1/3 pg. vertical

8 1/2x11 vertical

Illustrations on this page by **David Graves,** *133 RR Wheeler St., Gloucester, MA 01930, 508-283-2335*

6x9 vertical

7x4 3/4, 1/2 pg. horizontal

7x10 vertical

2 3/8x10, 1/3 pg. vertical

8 1/2x11 vertical

The following 24 pages show examples of color photogra-phy covering one-half the design area. They present opportunities to combine type within the photograph with type in the open space. The photographs on this page are by **Rob Huntley,** *Chromographics, Inc., 9 May St., Beverly, MA 01915, 508-927-7451*

7x4 3/4, 1/2 pg. horizontal

6x9 vertical

7x10 vertical

2 3/8x10, 1/3 pg. vertical

8 1/2x11 vertical

Photographs on this page by **White/Packert Photography,**
107 South St., Boston, MA 02111, 617-423-0577

6x9 vertical

7x4 3/4, 1/2 pg. horizontal

7x10 vertical

2 3/8x10, 1/3 pg. vertical

8 1/2x11 vertical

Photographs on this page by **Paul Avis,** *603-627-2659,*
FAX 603-627-4854
Represented by Jane Sutton

6x9 vertical

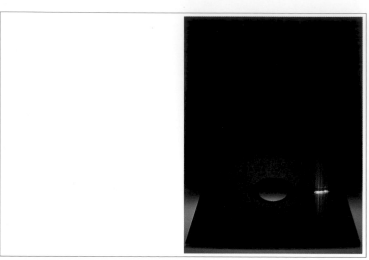

7x4 3/4, 1/2 pg. horizontal

7x10 vertical

2 3/8x10, 1/3 pg. vertical

8 1/2x11 vertical

Photographs on this page by **SuperStock,** *11 West 19th St., New York, NY 10011, 212-633-0300*

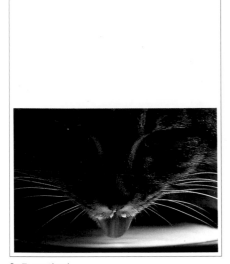

7x4 3/4, 1/2 pg. horizontal

0x0 vertical

7x10 vertical

2 3/8x10, 1/3 pg. vertical

8 1/2x11 vertical

Photographs on this page by **Eric Roth Studio,**
337 Summer St., Boston, MA 02210, 617-338-5358
Janet K. Henderson, Manager

7x4 3/4, 1/2 pg. horizontal

6x9 vertical

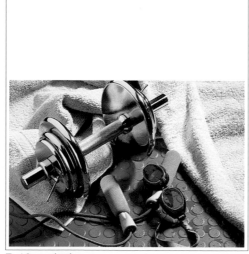

7x10 vertical

2 3/8x10, 1/3 pg. vertical

8 1/2x11 vertical

Photographs on this page by **Sandro Miller,** *New View Studios, 5275 Michigan Ave., Rosemont, IL 60018, 708-671-0300*
Represented by Elizabeth Miller

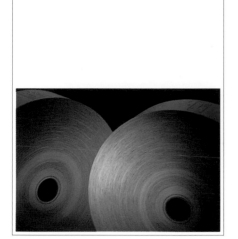

8x9 vertical

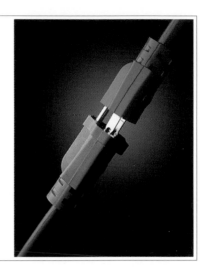

7x4 3/4, 1/2 pg. horizontal

7x10 vertical

2 3/8x10, 1/3 pg. vertical

8 1/2x11 vertical

Photographs on this page by **Scott Payne,** *New View Studios, 5275 Michigan Ave., Rosemont, IL 60018, 708-671-0300*
Represented by Elizabeth Miller

7x4 3/4, 1/2 pg. horizontal

6x9 vertical

7x10 vertical

2 3/8x10, 1/3 pg. vertical

8 1/2x11 vertical

Photographs on this page by **Terence O'Toole,**
Panorama Productions, 118 Social Hall Avenue,
Salt Lake City, UT 84111, 801-364-7482

8x9 vertical

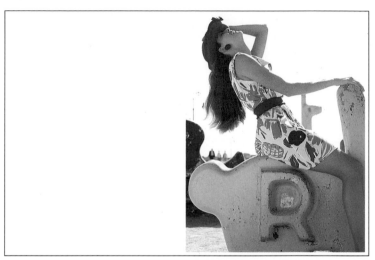

7x4 3/4, 1/2 pg. horizontal

7x10 vertical

2 3/8x10, 1/3 pg. vertical

8 1/2x11 vertical

Photographs on this page by **Rod Cook,** *New York, NY,*
212-995-0100
Represented by Terry Dagrosa, 212-254-4254

6x9 vertical

7x4 3/4, 1/2 pg. horizontal

7x10 vertical

2 3/8x10, 1/3 pg. vertical

8 1/2x11 vertical

Photographs on this page by **Dennis Gray** *, 8705 W. Washington Blvd., Culver City, CA 90232, 213-559-1711*

7x4 3/4, 1/2 pg. horizontal

6x0 vertical

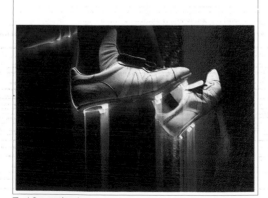

7x10 vertical

2 3/8x10, 1/3 pg. vertical

8 1/2x11 vertical

Photographs on this page by **Rob Van Petten,** *109 Broad St., Boston, MA 02110, 617-426-8641*

7x4 3/4, 1/2 pg. horizontal

6x9 vertical

7x10 vertical

2 3/8x10, 1/3 pg. vertical   8 1/2x11 vertical

Photographs on this page by **John Huet Photography,**
27 Drydock Avenue, Boston MA 02210
617-439-9393
Represented by Marilyn Cadenbach Associates
617-484-7437

7x4 3/4, 1/2 pg. horizontal

6x9 vertical

7x10 vertical

2 3/8x10, 1/3 pg. vertical

8 1/2x11 vertical

Photographs on this page by **Benoit Photography,** *31 Blackburn Center, Gloucester, MA 01930, 508-281-3079*

7x4 3/4, 1/2 pg. horizontal

6x9 vertical

7x10 vertical

2 3/8x10, 1/3 pg. vertical

8 1/2x11 vertical

Photographs on this page by **Ken Sabatini,** *1112 Beachwood Dr., Los Angeles, CA 90038, 213-462-7744*

6x9 vertical

7x4 3/4, 1/2 pg. horizontal

7x10 vertical

2 3/8x10, 1/3 pg. vertical

8 1/2x11 vertical

The photos on this page are by **SuperStock,**
11 West 19th St., N.Y., N.Y. 10011, 212-633-0300

7x4 3/4, 1/2 pg. horizontal

6x9 vertical

7x10 vertical

2 3/8x10, 1/3 pg. vertical

8 1/2x11 vertical

Photographs on this page by **Wayne Calabrese,** *CR2 Studios Inc., 36 St. Paul St., 601/The Cox Building, Rochester, NY 14604, 716-232-5140*

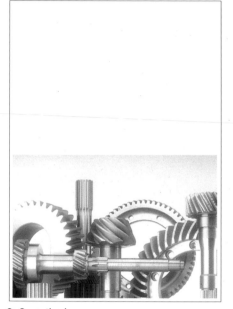

6x9 vertical

7x4 3/4, 1/2 pg. horizontal

7x10 vertical

2 3/8x10, 1/3 pg. vertical

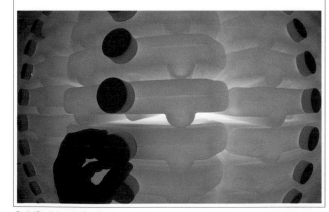

8 1/2x11 vertical

Photographs on this page by **Lorraine Parow,** *Toronto, CANADA, 416-461-3847*

7x4 3/4, 1/2 pg. horizontal

6x9 vertical

7x10 vertical

2 3/8x10, 1/3 pg. vertical   8 1/2x11 vertical

Photographs on this page by **Clint Clemens.**
Represented by A Corporation for Art and Commerce,
212-206-0737, FAX 212-463-7267

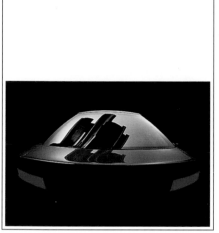

7x4 3/4, 1/2 pg. horizontal

8x9 vertical

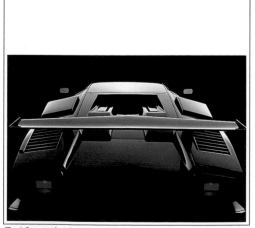

7x10 vertical

2 3/8x10, 1/3 pg. vertical

8 1/2x11 vertical

TYPE IN PLACE

Photographs on this page by **John Huet Photography,**
27 Drydock Avenue, Boston MA 02210
617-439-9393
Represented by Marilyn Cadenbach Associates
617-484-7437

6x9 vertical

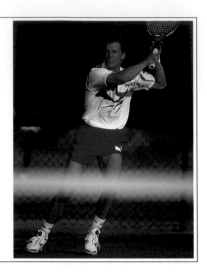

7x4 3/4, 1/2 pg. horizontal

7x10 vertical

2 3/8x10, 1/3 pg. vertical

8 1/2x11 vertical

Photographs on this page by **SuperStock,** *11 West 19th St., New York, NY 10011, 212-633-0300*

6x9 vertical

7x4 3/4, 1/2 pg. horizontal

7x10 vertical

2 3/8x10, 1/3 pg. vertical

8 1/2x11 vertical

Photographs on this page by **SuperStock,** *11 West 19th St., New York, NY 10011, 212-633-0300*

7x4 3/4, 1/2 pg. horizontal

6x9 vertical

7x10 vertical

2 3/8x10, 1/3 pg. vertical

8 1/2x11 vertical

Photographs on this page by **Susie Cushner Photography,** *354 Congress Street, Boston, MA 02210, 617-542-4070*
Represented by Marilyn Cadenbach Associates 617-484-7437

7x4 3/4, 1/2 pg. horizontal

6x9 vertical

7x10 vertical

2 3/8x10, 1/3 pg. vertical

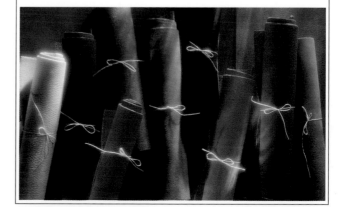

8 1/2x11 vertical

Photographs on this page by **Geoffrey Stein Studio, Inc.,** *348 Newbury Street, Boston, MA 02115 617-536-8227*

7x4 3/4, 1/2 pg. horizontal

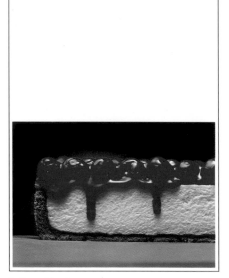

6x9 vertical

7x10 vertical

2 3/8x10, 1/3 pg. vertical

8 1/2x11 vertical

Photographs on this page by **Susie Cushner Photography,** *354 Congress Street, Boston MA 02210*
617-542-4070
Represented by Marilyn Cadenbach Associates
617-484-7437

6x9 vertical

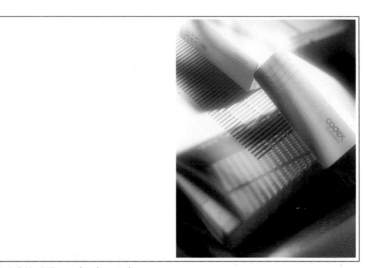

7x4 3/4, 1/2 pg. horizontal

7x10 vertical

2 3/8x10, 1/3 pg. vertical

8 1/2x11 vertical

The following 8 pages show examples of color photography covering one-fourth the design area. They present opportunities to combine type within the photograph with type in the open space. The photographs on these 8 pages are by **SuperStock,** *11 West 19th St., New York, NY 10011, 212-633-0300*

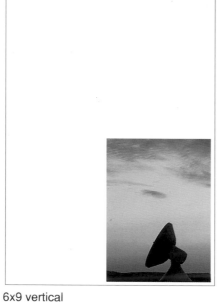

6x9 vertical

7x4 3/4, 1/2 pg. horizontal

7x10 vertical

2 3/8x10, 1/3 pg. vertical

8 1/2x11 vertical

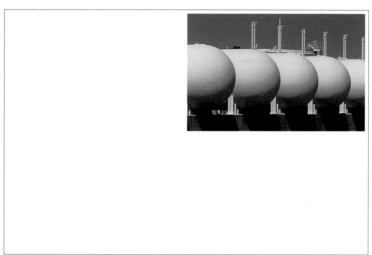

7x4 3/4, 1/2 pg. horizontal

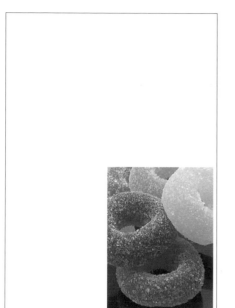

6x9 vertical

7x10 vertical

2 3/8x10, 1/3 pg. vertical

8 1/2x11 vertical

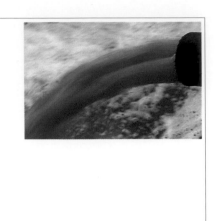

6x9 vertical

7x4 3/4, 1/2 pg. horizontal

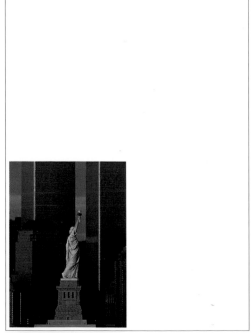

7x10 vertical

2 3/8x10, 1/3 pg. vertical

8 1/2x11 vertical

7x4 3/4, 1/2 pg. horizontal

6x9 vertical

7x10 vertical

2 3/8x10, 1/3 pg. vertical   8 1/2x11 vertical

7x4 3/4, 1/2 pg. horizontal

6x9 vertical

7x10 vertical

2 3/8x10, 1/3 pg. vertical

8 1/2x11 vertical

7x4 3/4, 1/2 pg. horizontal

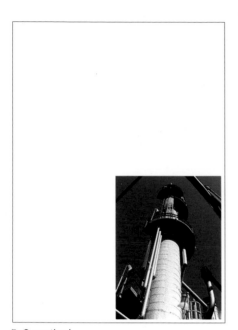

6x0 vertical

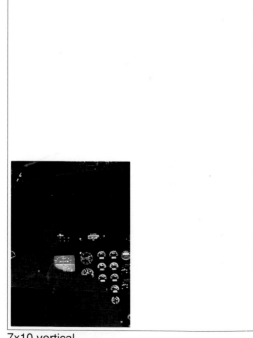

7x10 vertical

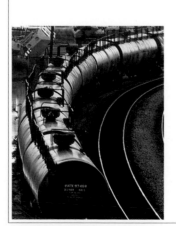

2 3/8x10, 1/3 pg. vertical   8 1/2x11 vertical

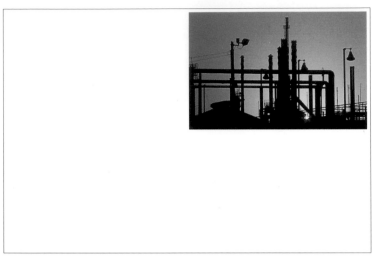

7x4 3/4, 1/2 pg. horizontal

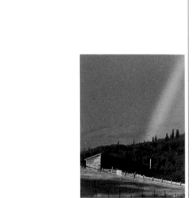

6x9 vertical

7x10 vertical

2 3/8x10, 1/3 pg. vertical

8 1/2x11 vertical

7x4 3/4, 1/2 pg. horizontal

6x9 vertical

7x10 vertical

2 3/8x10, 1/3 pg. vertical   8 1/2x11 vertical

The following eight pages show examples of full coverage of solid color. They present opportunities for both black overprinted and white reverse type. Next to each rectangle is a breakdown of the combination of process colors used. (c=cyan, m=magenta, y=yellow)

100c, 5m, 20y

6x9 vertical

60c, 5m, 20y

7x4 3/4, 1/2 pg. horizontal

40c, 5m, 20y

7x10 vertical

20c, 5m, 20y

2 3/8x10, 1/3 pg. vertical

5c, 5m, 20y

8 1/2x11 vertical

60c, 60m, 90y

6x9 vertical

40c, 40m, 70y

7x4 3/4, 1/2 pg. horizontal

30c, 30m, 60y

7x10 vertical

20c, 20m, 50y

2 3/8x10, 1/3 pg. vertical

10c, 10m, 40y

8 1/2x11 vertical

60c, 60m, 60y

40c, 40m, 40y

7x4 3/4, 1/2 pg. horizontal

6x9 vertical

30c, 30m, 30y

20c, 20m, 20y

10c, 10m, 10y

7x10 vertical

2 3/8x10, 1/3 pg. vertical

8 1/2x11 vertical

30c, 100y

6x9 vertical

30c, 60y

7x4 3/4, 1/2 pg. horizontal

30c, 20y

30c, 5y

30c, 40y

7x10 vertical

2 3/8x10, 1/3 pg. vertical

8 1/2x11 vertical

100c, 20m, 100y

6x9 vertical

60c, 20m, 100y

7x4 3/4, 1/2 pg. horizontal

40c, 20m, 100y

7x10 vertical

20c, 20m, 100y

2 3/8x10, 1/3 pg. vertical

5c, 20m, 100y

8 1/2x11 vertical

100c, 5m, 60y

6x9 vertical

60c, 5m, 60y

7x4 3/4, 1/2 pg. horizontal

5c, 5m, 60y

40c, 5m, 60y

20c, 5m, 60y

7x10 vertical

2 3/8x10, 1/3 pg. vertical

8 1/2x11 vertical

40c, 100m

6x9 vertical

40c, 60m

7x4 3/4, 1/2 pg. horizontal

40c, 40m

7x10 vertical

40c, 20m

2 3/8x10, 1/3 pg. vertical

40c, 5m

8 1/2x11 vertical

1C0c, 20m, 40y

6x9 vertical

60c, 20m, 40y

7x4 3/4, 1/2 pg. horizontal

40c, 20m, 40y

7x10 vertical

20c, 20m, 40y

2 3/8x10, 1/3 pg. vertical

5c, 20m, 40y

8 1/2x11 vertical

The following four pages show examples of solid color covering one-half the design area. They present opportunities to combine type within the color area with type in the open space. (c=cyan, m=magenta, y=yellow)

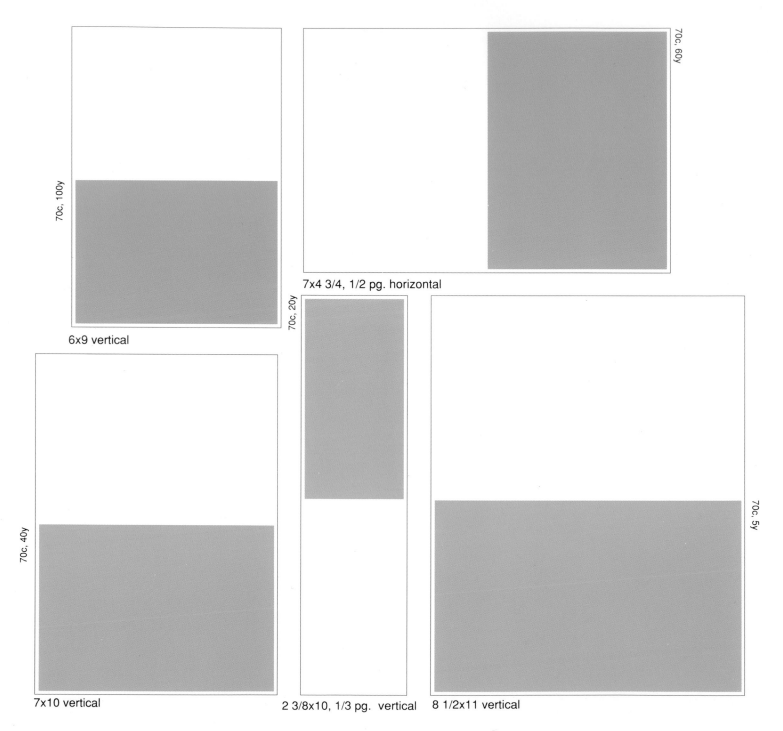

70c, 100y

6x9 vertical

70c, 60y

7x4 3/4, 1/2 pg. horizontal

70c, 40y

7x10 vertical

70c, 20y

2 3/8x10, 1/3 pg. vertical

70c, 5y

8 1/2x11 vertical

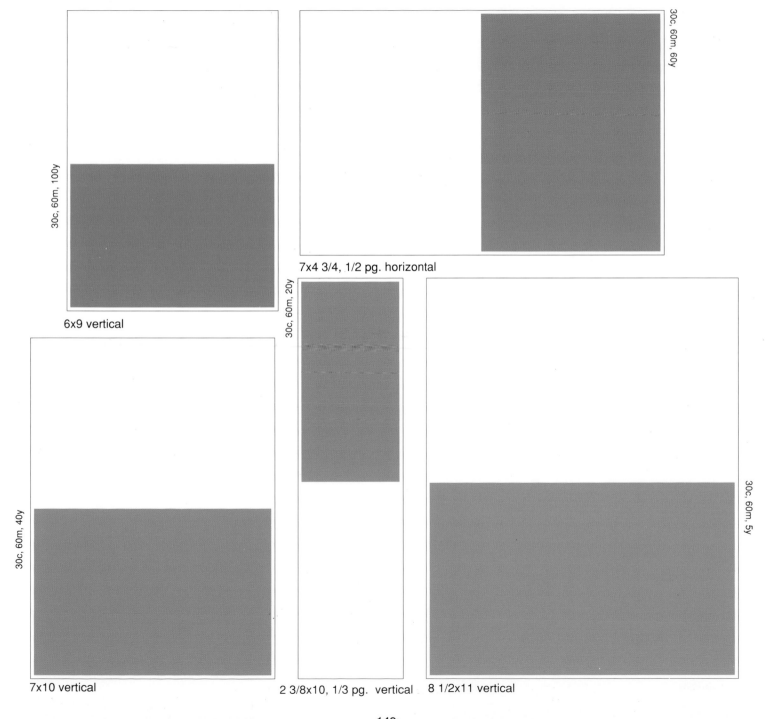

30c, 60m, 60y

30c, 60m, 100y

6x9 vertical

7x4 3/4, 1/2 pg. horizontal

30c, 60m, 20y

30c, 60m, 40y

30c, 60m, 5y

7x10 vertical

2 3/8x10, 1/3 pg. vertical

8 1/2x11 vertical

The following two pages show examples of full coverage of solid color. They present opportunities for both black over-printed type and white reverse type. Next to each rectangle is a breakdown of the combination of process colors used. (c=cyan, m=magenta, y=yellow)

100c, 5m, 20y

6x9 vertical

60c, 5m, 20y

7x4 3/4, 1/2 pg. horizontal

40c, 5m, 20y

7x10 vertical

20c, 5m, 20y

2 3/8x10, 1/3 pg. vertical

5c, 5m, 20y

8 1/2x11 vertical

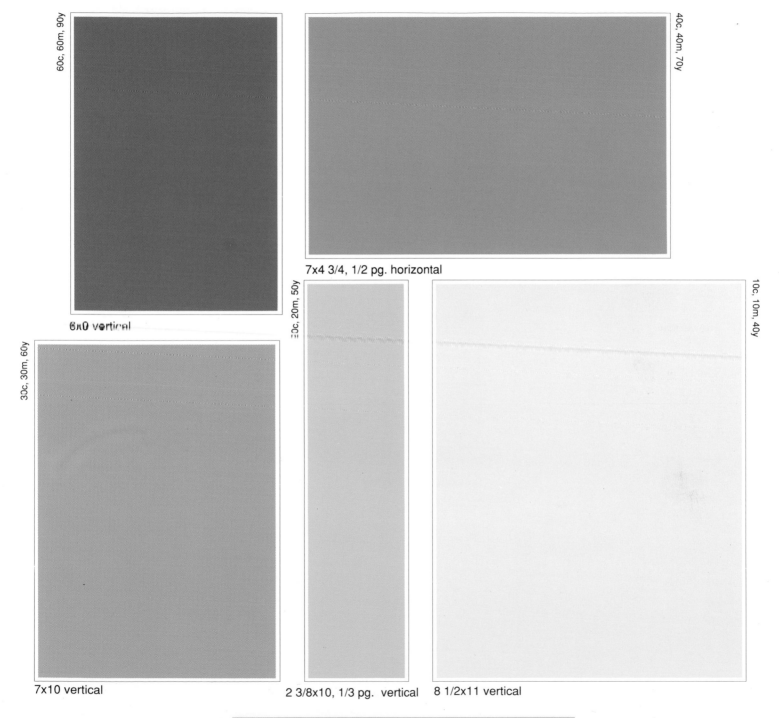

60c, 60m, 90y

40c, 40m, 70y

7x4 3/4, 1/2 pg. horizontal

6x9 vertical

30c, 30m, 60y

30c, 20m, 50y

10c, 10m, 40y

7x10 vertical

2 3/8x10, 1/3 pg. vertical

8 1/2x11 vertical

The following two pages show examples of solid color covering one-half the design area. They present opportunities to combine type within the color area with type in the open space. (c=cyan, m=magenta, y=yellow)

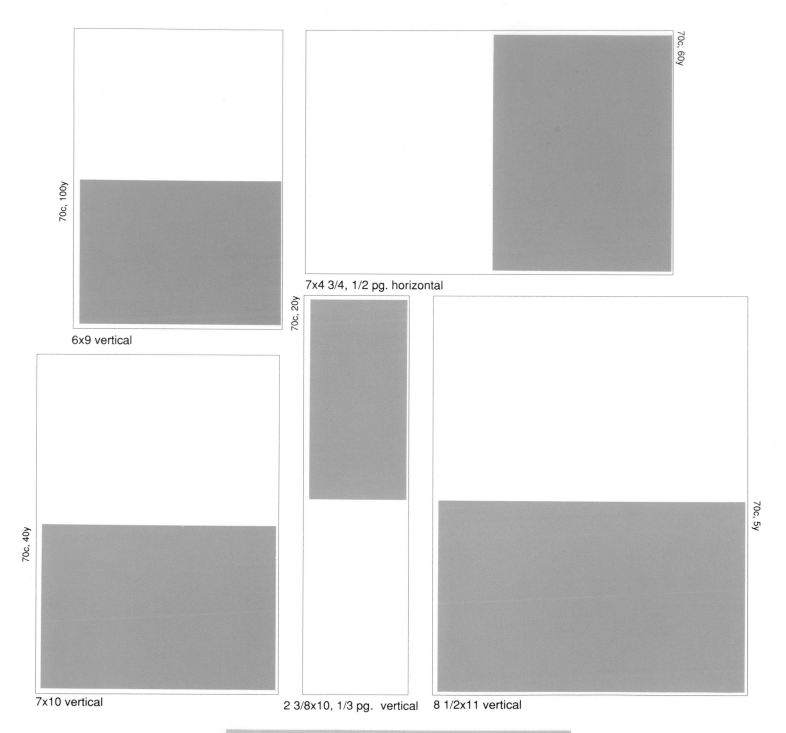

70c, 100y

70c, 60y

6x9 vertical

7x4 3/4, 1/2 pg. horizontal

70c, 20y

70c, 40y

70c, 5y

7x10 vertical

2 3/8x10, 1/3 pg. vertical

8 1/2x11 vertical

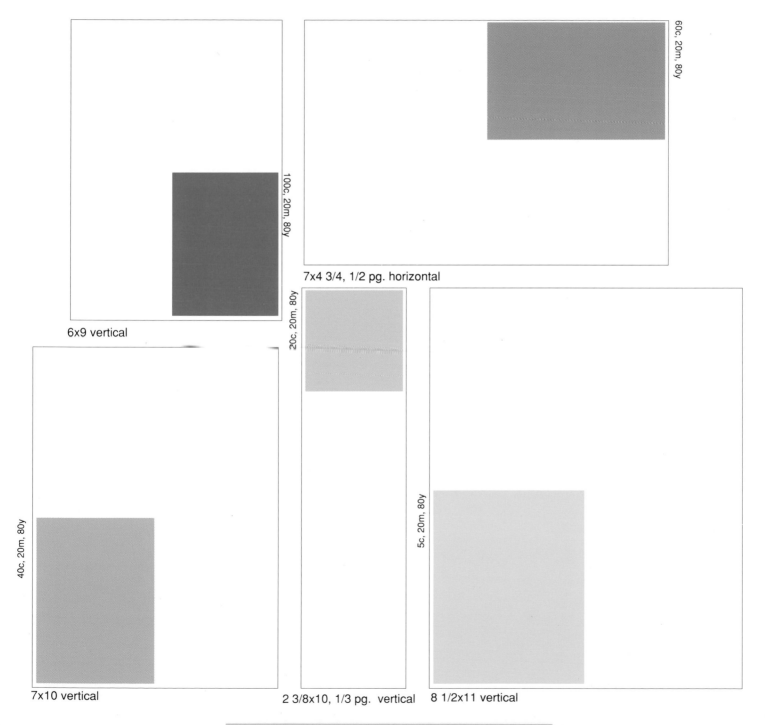

60c, 20m, 80y

100c, 20m, 80y

7x4 3/4, 1/2 pg. horizontal

6x9 vertical

20c, 20m, 80y

40c, 20m, 80y

5c, 20m, 80y

7x10 vertical

2 3/8x10, 1/3 pg. vertical

8 1/2x11 vertical

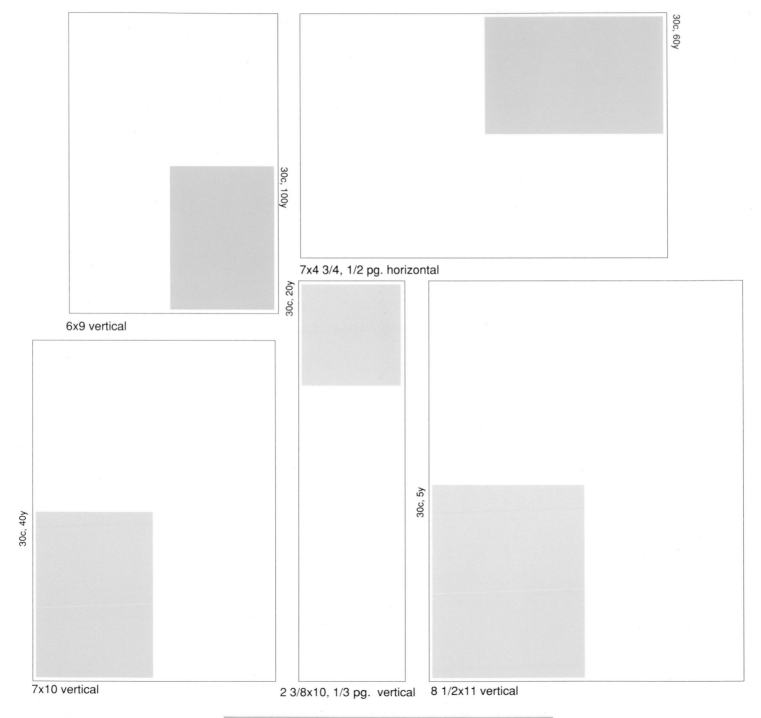

30c, 60y

30c, 100y

7x4 3/4, 1/2 pg. horizontal

6x9 vertical

30c, 20y

30c, 40y

30c, 5y

7x10 vertical

2 3/8x10, 1/3 pg. vertical

8 1/2x11 vertical

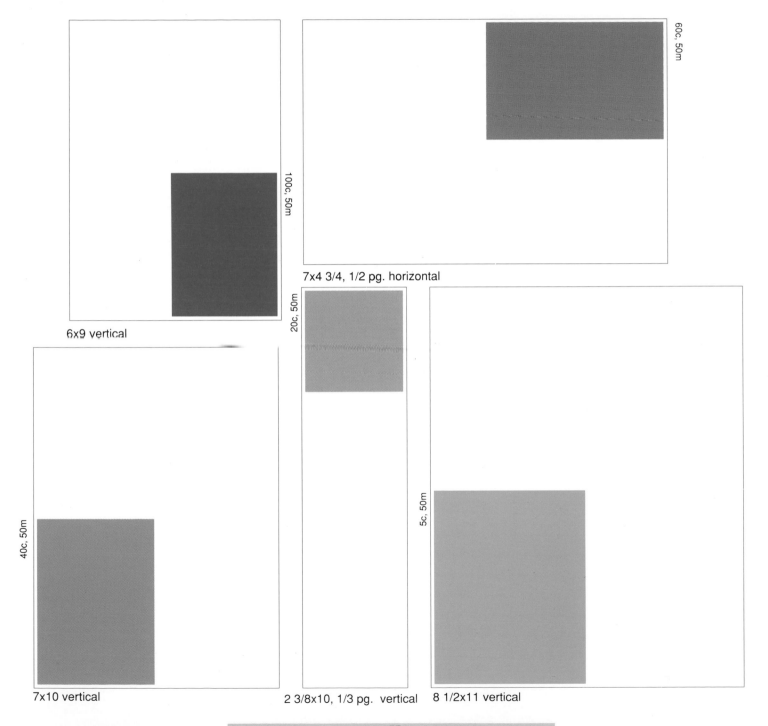

6x9 vertical

100c, 50m

60c, 50m

7x4 3/4, 1/2 pg. horizontal

20c, 50m

40c, 50m

5c, 50m

7x10 vertical

2 3/8x10, 1/3 pg. vertical

8 1/2x11 vertical

PHOTO AND ILLUSTRATION CREDITS

7: R. Llewellyn. 13: R. Llewellyn. 60: (clockwise from top left) Rivera Collection, R. Lee, R. Chen, GALA, S. Barrow. 61: (clockwise from top left) B. Apton, C. Orrico, S. Barrow, S. Barrow, F. Wood. 62-63: Rob Huntley. 64-65: White/Packert. 66-67: Eric Roth. 68-69: Terence O'Toole. 70-71: Paul Avis. 72-73: David Benoit. 74-75: Sandro Miller. 76-77: Scott Payne. 78-79: Rod Cook. 80-81: Rob Van Petten. 82-83: Dennis Gray. 84-85: Ken Sabatini. 86: (clockwise from top left) S. Barrow, R. Llewellyn, Rivera Collection, BL PRODUCTIONS, Rivera Collection. 87: (clockwise from top left) G. Kullenberg, Rivera Collection, M. Romine, R. Heinzen, M. Keller. 88-89: Lorraine Parow. 90-91: Wayne Calabrese. 92-93: Clint Clemens. 94-95: Susie Cushner. 96-97: John Huet. 98-99: Joeff Stein. 100: (clockwise from top left) R. Heinzen, G. Outerbridge, K. Kitagawa, F. Wood, Rivera Collection. 101: (clockwise from top left) R. Heinzen, Rivera Collection, R. Llewellyn, A. Briere, Rivera Collection. 102: Gaylord Welker. 103: Kirk Moldoff. 104: Dick Palulian. 105: Bob Conge. 106: Gary Ruddell. 107: David Graves. 108: Rob Huntley. 109: White/Packert. 110: Paul Avis. 111: (clockwise from top left) J. Amos, Ong. & Assoc., Rivera Collection, GALA, G. Outerbridge. 112: Eric Roth. 113: Sandro Miller. 114: Scott Payne. 115: Terence O'Toole. 116: Rod Cook. 117: Dennis Gray. 118: Rob Van Petten. 119: John Huet. 120: David Benoit. 121: Ken Sabatini. 122: (clockwise from top left) R. Heinzen, J. DeSelliers, Rivera Collection, R. Dahlquist, Rivera Collection. 123: Lorraine Parow. 124: Wayne Calabrese. 125: Clint Clemens. 126: John Huet. 127: (clockwise from top left) P. Van Rhijn, M. Roessler, Rivera Collection, C. Orrico, T. Rosenthal. 128 : (clockwise from top left) R. Llewellyn, R. Llewellyn, R. Lee, R. Dahlquist, R. Heinzen. 129: Susie Cushner. 130: Joeff Stein. 131: Susie Cushner. 132: (clockwise from top left) S. Vidler, R. Heinzen, S. Barrow, D. Spindel, M. Regan. 133: (clockwise from top left) Rivera Collection, Fletcher Col., D. Harvey, R. Llewellyn, R. Llewellyn. 134: (clockwise from top left) R. Heinzen, H. Pelletier, L. Dunmire, R. Dahlquist, S.Barrow. 135: (clockwise from top left) Glod Collection, Ong. & Assoc., R. Dahlquist, G. Kullenberg, L. Radeka. 136: (clockwise from top left) R. Heinzen, R. Heinzen, M. Fife, R. Dahlquist, R. Llewellyn. 137: (clockwise from top left) R. Llewellyn, R. Llewellyn, W. Woodworth, A. Briere, J. Atnip. 138: (clockwise from top left) R. Dahlquist, GALA, R. Van Rhijn, Rivera Collection, Ong. & Assoc. 139: (clockwise from top left) Shostal, R. Llewellyn, M. Romine, S. Barrow, R. Lee.

ALSO AVAILABLE FROM ROCKPORT PUBLISHERS

Rockport Publishers Inc., P.O. Box 396, 5 Smith Street, Rockport, MA 01966 Phone: (508)546-9590
Fax: (508) 546-7141

TYPE & COLOR

TYPE & COLOR eliminates the guesswork, allowing you to test more than 800,000 combinations of typefaces, sizes, and colors, before you go to press. You get 100 pages of carefully selected color bands to use with eleven sheets of clear acetate. The acetates are printed with eight typefaces in three sizes and varying colors (eighteen colors in all). One sheet of acetate has a gray scale in six densities ranging from 10% to 70% so you can also preview grayed colors. Also included are examples of great uses of type & color. An examination of color theory and ideas make this your complete color guide.

160 pages and 11 acetates   **ISBN 0-935603-19-0**
$39.95   **Hardcover**

DESIGNS FOR MARKETING NO. 1: PRIMO ANGELI

Journey with this premier graphic designer as he traces the development of his well-known commercial designs - including DHL, TreeSweet, Cambridge, Henry Weinhard beer, California Cooler- from initial client meetings to the finished designs. Packed with more than 300 four-color photographs and accompanied by lively text, this is an essential reference for graphic artists and marketers.

144 pages   **ISBN 0-935603-65-4**
$19.95   **Softcover**

THE GUILD 6
2 VOLUMES

Volume One, THE ARCHITECT'S SOURCE: The only sourcebook of its kind, The Guild displays the work of North America's finest craft artists who do architectural installations. The Guild presents over 200 artists working in architectural glass, metal, wood, and stone. Volume Two, THE DESIGNER'S SOURCE: One of the most prestigious juried showcases for North American crafts. Included are hand-made furniture, accessories, and wall hangings in a variety of media. The Guild features the best hand-crafted furnishings for the home or office.

Volume One 200 pages ($24.95)ISBN 0-9616012-6-4
Volume Two 336 pages ($34.95) ISBN 0-9616012-8-0
Two Volume set in slipcase ($59.95)

THE BEST IN MEDICAL ADVERTISING AND GRAPHICS

Four hundred stunning and remarkably ingenious medical ads and illustrations have been brought together in this book. This must-have reference captures, in full-color, the astonishing creativity of a group of graphic arts specialists whose work has never been seen in such entirety. THE BEST IN MEDICAL ADVERTISING AND GRAPHICS not only displays the exceptional graphic techniques of the industries' top creative talents, but also presents the effort behind the ads. Included is information on advertising goals and strategies, design objectives, audience targeting and clients' restrictions.

256 pages   **ISBN 0-935603-20-4**
$49.95   **Hardcover**

THE BEST OF SCREEN PRINTING DESIGN

The first major book devoted to the graphic rather than functional aspects of screen printing captures the elegance and utility of this important art form. The book contains superb screen print designs of limited edition art, garments, textiles, vinyl goods and posters, all reproduced in vibrant color. Each illustration is accompanied by information on design strategy, marketing and technical details.

256 pages   **ISBN 0-935603-17-4**
$49.95   **Hardcover**

COLOR HARMONY

A step-by-step guide to choosing and combining colors, COLOR HARMONY includes 1,662 individual color combinations; dozens of full-color photos to show you how your color schemes will look; a four-color conversion chart; 61 full-size color charts and much more.

158 pages   **ISBN 0-935603-06-9**
$15.95   **Softcover**

COLOR SOURCEBOOK I

Originally published with great success in Japan, COLOR SOURCEBOOK I is a treasure trove of ideas for creating color combinations, shapes, and patterns. Color concepts under the headings 'Natural', 'Oriental', and 'High-Tech' provide interesting and useful color design combinations to help create an appropriate color framework for the designer to work within. Instructions are specific, geared toward the professional, yet clear enough to be useful to the student.

112 pages   **ISBN 0-935603-28-X**
$15.95   **Softcover**

COLOR SOURCEBOOK II

Today color and design go hand in hand, and for this reason, COLOR SOURCEBOOK II is an indispensable tool for creating color combinations, shapes and patterns. This second essential volume furnishes the designer with color concepts uner the headings 'Pop', 'Retro-Modern', and 'Post Modern', and creates color and design fields for the designer to work within.

112 pages   **ISBN 0-935603-29**
$15.95   **Softcover**

A TYPEFACE SOURCEBOOK

This is much more than a type book. With 1488 unscreened full alphabets shown on 672 pages, this is the photolettering industry's most up-to-date and comprehensive typeface reference book. A TYPEFACE SOURCEBOOK includes an extensive spacing guide and is cross-indexed, with 82 pages of one-liners arranged both alphabetically and categorically. The smyth binding allows the book to lay flat for reproduction. This book is an essential working tool for all graphic professionals. A comprehensive introduction explains everyday use, giving the reader complete access to the typefaces enclosed.

672 pages   **ISBN 0-935603-47-6**
$39.95   **Softcover**

VOLUME ONE: TRADEMARKS & SYMBOLS OF THE WORLD
THE ALPHABET IN DESIGN

This wonderful resource and idea book presents more than 1,700 contemporary designs from a variety of sources for every letter of the alphabet. An essential resource for anyone involved in typography, sign and logo design and creating corporate identities.

192 pages   **ISBN 4-7601-0451-8**
$24.95   **Softcover**

VOLUME TWO: TRADEMARKS & SYMBOLS OF THE WORLD
DESIGN ELEMENTS

If you design packages, ads, corporate logos, or signage, you must have this resource guide in your design library. It features more than 1,700 design elements that can add pizzazz to any printed piece.

192 pages   **ISBN 4-7601-0450-X**
$24.95   **Softcover**

VOLUME THREE: TRADEMARKS & SYMBOLS OF THE WORLD
PICTOGRAM AND SIGN DISIGN

Includes pictogram and sign design from all over the world, which nonverbally convey an incredible variety of messages, symbols, ideas, and identities. It also includes detailed information on the background of each design, including business category, art director, client, year and place designed. This is a must-have volume for the graphic designer.

232 pages   **ISBN 0-935603-30-1**
$24.95   **Softcover**